VEGETARIAN COOKING AROUND THE WORLD

Lerner Publications Company
A division of Lerner Publishing Group
241 First Avenue North
Minneapolis, MN 55401 U.S.A.

Website address: www.lernerbooks.com

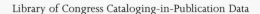

Library of Congress Cataloging-in-Publication Data

Behnke, Alison.
    Vegetarian cooking around the world / compiled by Alison Behnke.
— Rev. and expanded.
          p.   cm. — (Easy menu ethnic cookbooks)
    ISBN: 0–8225–4130–0 (lib. bdg. : alk. paper)
    ISBN: 0–8225–0514–2 (pbk. : alk. paper)
    1. Vegetarian cookery—Juvenile literature. 2. Cookery, International—Juvenile literature. [1. Vegetarian cookery. 2. Cookery, International.]
I. Title. II. Series.
TX837 .B397 2002
641.5'636—dc21   2001004241

Manufactured in the United States of America
1 2 3 4 5 6 – AM – 07 06 05 04 03 02

VEGETARIAN

revised and expanded

COOKING

to include new

AROUND THE

low-fat recipes

WORLD

compiled by Alison Behnke

Lerner Publications Company • Minneapolis

Contents

Introduction

Vegetarian cooking is nothing new. People in many cultures have enjoyed vegetarian or mostly vegetarian meals for generations. However, vegetarianism is growing in popularity. In modern times, more and more people around the world are recognizing the health benefits of omitting or reducing meat in their diets. An increasing number of tasty, healthy alternatives to meat, such as tofu, tempeh, seitan, and a variety of veggie burgers and veggie dogs, are available in supermarkets and groceries. Many cooks and diners enjoy exploring and discovering foods from other nations, some of which use little or no meat. All of these factors have led to a new approach to vegetarian dining. By making good use of a wide range of ingredients, creative seasoning, varied cooking techniques, and recipes from international cuisines, modern cooks are finding that vegetarian cooking offers a wealth of dishes that are versatile and delicious.

Chinese New Year's noodles get the year off to a tasty start with crunchy veggies and the zing of fresh ginger. (Recipe on page 66.)

Vegetarianism around the World

Vegetarianism is the practice of not eating meat, fish, or poultry. Some vegetarians, called vegans, also exclude eggs, milk, and other animal products from their diets. Others who consider themselves vegetarian avoid red meat but eat poultry, fish, or both.

Attitudes about meat-centered meals often stem from the culture in which people live. People get used to eating certain foods and not others. For example, in contrast to North America, Australia, and Europe, where most people eat meat, most people in India are vegetarians. In other parts of the world, such as regions of Africa and China, meat may be an unaffordable luxury for the average person.

People are vegetarians for many reasons. Some choose vegetarianism because of personal ethical or moral views, believing that it is wrong to kill animals for meat. Others believe it is unhealthy to eat meat. Certain religious groups, such as Hindus and many Buddhists, practice vegetarianism as part of their faith. Still others are concerned that the earth's ability to feed its population is limited. Worldwide, good agricultural land is scarce, and a large portion of this limited resource is used to grow grain that is fed to cattle. Some people believe that it would make more sense to use that land to grow crops for human consumption.

Vegetarian Nutrition

Although vegetarianism can be a very healthy lifestyle, vegetarians must be sure that their bodies are getting the necessary nutrients. For example, children need a certain amount of protein in their diets in order to grow properly, and everyone needs protein to remain healthy. Meat and dairy products are excellent sources of protein, but they are not the only sources. Fruits, vegetables, grains, and legumes (plants that grow seeds within pods, such as beans, peas, and lentils) also provide protein. However, most plant proteins are not complete proteins—proteins that contain all of the necessary amino acids, the building blocks of protein. Soybeans and soybean products such as tofu and soy milk do contain complete proteins, making them very popular among vegetarians. But eating certain combinations of other foods in the same meal, or even in the same day or two, can also supply the body with complete proteins. These combinations include beans, lentils, or peanuts with rice, wheat, or corn. For example, rice and lentils, corn tortillas and beans, and even peanut butter and wheat bread all provide complete proteins.

Calcium is another necessary part of a balanced diet that is provided by animal products, primarily dairy. Calcium is very important for healthy bones, joints, and teeth. However, many meatless and nondairy foods contain significant amounts of calcium. Whole grains, legumes, nuts, and dark green vegetables such as broccoli and kale are all good vegetarian sources of calcium.

The most important thing to remember when considering a vegetarian diet is balance. A healthy assortment of fruits, vegetables, and grains can provide most of the vitamins and minerals that the body needs, without adding much fat or cholesterol.

Holidays and Festivals

Cultures around the world celebrate special occasions with special foods. Sharing a holiday or festival meal with friends and family is a tradition shared by people of all backgrounds, beliefs, and lifestyles. Many holiday meals can be simply adapted to a vegetarian diet, while other traditional feasts and festivities focus on foods or dishes that are vegetarian to begin with. No matter what the event, the vegetarian diner can easily celebrate with a sumptuous meal.

Many Jewish holidays feature vegetarian dishes. Some of these foods symbolize events in Jewish history. For example, Passover cake is made with matzo, a flat, unleavened bread representing the hardships endured by Hebrews in ancient Egypt and the last meal

Hebrew families shared before they fled from Egypt to escape slavery. Kosher dining—eating according to rules stated in religious documents—also influences Jewish holiday foods. One rule forbids eating meat and milk together, which can result in meals that are meatless but rich in dairy products. Shavuot, the holiday in remembrance of the Biblical figure Moses receiving the Torah (a holy book of the Jewish faith), is celebrated with a variety of dairy foods, while meat and fish are avoided. A popular dish at this celebration is blintzes—thin pancakes filled with cottage cheese or farmers' cheese.

Dietary rules also govern the followers of Hinduism. Most Hindus don't eat any meat, so many of the foods of their special occasions are vegetarian. In India, treats for the luminous Diwali (the Hindu festival of lights) include khir, a sweet rice pudding prepared with

A mother and son celebrate Diwali (the Hindu festival of lights) by lighting candles and sparklers in Kolkata (formerly Calcutta), India.

rice, milk, nuts, and an array of spices; and *halva*, which is a rich dessert made with butter, grated vegetables, chopped nuts, honey, and dried fruit. The Holi festival, celebrating the arrival of spring, features *puran poli*, sweet stuffed bread made with beans or lentils; *gujjia*, deep-fried pastries filled with nuts or raisins; and *samosas*, flaky crusts filled with spicy curried potatoes.

Like Hindus, Muslims (followers of Islam) obey a set of rules regarding diet. Some meat is allowed, but many Muslims believe that Muhammad, the founder of Islam, preferred to eat mostly vegetables and grains. During Ramadan, the holiest Islamic month, Muslims fast (neither eating nor drinking) from sunup to sundown. Meals during this month are simple and often meatless. Before dawn, a light breakfast such as porridge or bread and fruit is eaten. After dark, families share another meal which might include dates, bread, and soup. Eid al-Fitr marks the end of Ramadan, and many dishes at this feast are vegetarian. Spicy curried vegetables, hearty dishes of rice, potatoes, and lentils, and a range of sweets are enjoyed after the long fast.

Some Christian holidays also have long-standing vegetarian customs. Many Roman Catholics observe fasts, during which they may not eat any meat. The Polish Christmas Eve dinner, or Wigilia, is entirely meatless. Traditional dishes include borscht (beet soup), potatoes, and noodles with poppy seeds. Catholics in Italy also eat a meatless meal on Christmas Eve, enjoying pasta dishes and soups, though many cooks include fish on the menu. Other beloved foods of Christian holidays are sweets. In Germany, Christmas wouldn't be complete without a *stollen*, or fruit loaf, while in Mexico *buñuelos* are essential. These sweet fritters with cinnamon syrup are served on cracked or chipped plates, which diners break for good luck when they are finished eating. For Easter, bakers around the world prepare tempting breads, such as English hot cross buns (sweet buns with a white cross of icing) and Russian *kulich* (a tall, cylindrical sweet bread topped with white icing). Italians enjoy *colomba pasquale*, a dove-shaped bread studded with dried fruit or nuts, while Greeks celebrate with *tsouréki*, braided sweet bread decorated with hard-boiled eggs dyed red.

Many Asian countries have large Buddhist populations. Although not governed by strict dietary rules, some Buddhists are vegetarians. Others follow a vegetarian diet on certain days of the month, and many holiday dishes are meatless. One of the year's biggest events is the Lunar New Year, and a host of special food is associated with the festival. In Japan people eat *toshikoshi soba* ("year-crossing noodles") near midnight on Omisoka (New Year's Eve). Eating this soup with its extra-long, thin noodles as the new year begins is supposed to ensure long life. Long noodles are a popular dish for the Chinese New Year as well, and a must-have in Chinese homes is the traditional New Year's cake, made with sweet rice flour and decorated with festive red dates.

Many countries hold secular (non-religious) festivals dedicated to farming and food. Harvest festivals take place all over the globe, from the yam festival in the African nation of Ghana to sugarcane harvests in India and grain festivals in Europe. In Kenya the Masai celebrate the beginning of the rainy season in April with feasting, dancing, and singing. In Japan a whole calendar of ceremonies honors the planting, ripening, and harvesting of the rice crop.

No matter what the occasion or the country, food plays an important part in celebrations around the world. These events can be chances to participate in an old custom, expand culinary horizons, or create new food traditions. Whatever the case, the adventurous vegetarian diner need never look too far for a satisfying delicacy.

Planning the Menu

Planning a meatless menu offers great flexibility. Vegetarian meals may have a main entrée, or they may consist of two or three courses of equal importance. A vegetarian cook can serve a light meal of soup, bread, and salad, or for a heartier meal, a casserole or a pasta dish. Different combinations of flavors and textures provide variety, adding zest and contrast to any meal.

Young spectators watch festivities for the Festival of the Yam in Abengourou, Ivory Coast.

When planning your own menus, you may want to consider the seasons of the year. Serve a hot, thick soup on a cold winter night and perhaps a chilled fruit soup on a warm summer evening. Although imported produce may be available at all times of the year from almost any place in the world, certain fruits and vegetables are fresher and easier to find when they are at their peak. For example, crisp spears of asparagus appear in most markets in the spring, while summer brings sweet corn and bright red tomatoes. As a cook, you'll learn to enjoy taking advantage of fresh seasonal foods.

Adding an international flair to vegetarian meals offers a whole new world of flavors. The recipes in this book are a sampling from around the globe, representing more than a dozen countries, so step into the kitchen and explore some of the world's culinary treasures.

Before You Begin

The international recipes in this book call for some ingredients that you may not know. Sometimes special cookware is used, too, although these recipes can easily be prepared with ordinary utensils and pans.

The most important thing you need to know before you start is how to be a careful cook. On the following page, you'll find a few rules that will make your cooking experience safe, fun, and easy. Next, take a look at the "dictionary" of utensils, terms, and special ingredients. You may also want to read the list of tips on preparing healthy, low-fat meals.

When you've picked out a recipe to try, read through it from beginning to end. Now you are ready to shop for ingredients and to organize the cookware you will need. Once you have assembled everything, you're ready to begin cooking.

Refreshing bulgur salad (bottom) and creamy pumpkin soup (top) make a satisfying combination. (Recipes on pages 38 and 39.)

The Careful Cook

Whenever you cook, there are certain safety rules you must always keep in mind. Even experienced cooks follow these rules when they are in the kitchen.

- Always wash your hands before handling food. Thoroughly wash all raw vegetables and fruits to remove dirt, chemicals, and insecticides.
- Use a cutting board when cutting up vegetables and fruits. Don't cut them up in your hand! And be sure to cut in a direction *away* from you and your fingers.
- Long hair or loose clothing can easily catch fire if brought near the burners of a stove. If you have long hair, tie it back before you start cooking.
- Turn all pot handles toward the back of the stove so that you will not catch your sleeves or jewelry on them. This is especially important when younger brothers and sisters are around. They could easily knock off a pot and get burned.
- Always use a pot holder to steady hot pots or to take pans out of the oven. Don't use a wet cloth on a hot pan because the steam it produces could burn you.
- Lift the lid of a steaming pot with the opening away from you so that you will not get burned.
- If you get burned, hold the burn under cold running water. Do not put grease or butter on it. Cold water helps to take the heat out, but grease or butter will only keep it in.
- If grease or cooking oil catches fire, throw baking soda or salt at the bottom of the flame to put it out. (Water will *not* put out a grease fire.) Call for help, and try to turn all the stove burners to "off."

Cooking Utensils

colander—A bowl with holes in the bottom and sides. It is used for draining liquid from a solid food.

crepe pan—There are many pans available that are designed specifically for crepe-making, but almost any low-sided pan with a cooking surface 6 to 8 inches in diameter will work just as well.

rolling pin—A wooden utensil used for rolling out pastry or dough

sieve—A bowl-shaped utensil made of wire mesh used to drain food

slotted spoon—A spoon with small openings in the bowl. It is usually used to pick solid food out of a liquid.

spatula—A flat, thin utensil used to lift, toss, turn, or scoop up food

tongs—A utensil shaped either like tweezers or scissors with flat, blunt ends, used to grasp food

Cooking Terms

beat—To stir rapidly in a circular motion

boil—To heat a liquid over a high heat until bubbles form and rise rapidly to the surface

broil—To cook directly under a heat source so that the side of the food facing the heat cooks rapidly

chop—To cut into small pieces

grate—To shred food into tiny pieces by rubbing it against a grater

knead—To work dough by pressing it with the palms, pushing it outward and then pressing it over on itself

pinch—A very small amount, usually what you can pick up between your thumb and forefinger

preheat—To allow an oven to warm up to a certain temperature before putting food in it

sauté—To fry quickly over high heat in oil or fat, stirring or turning the food to prevent burning

simmer—To cook over low heat in liquid kept just below the boiling point. Bubbles will occasionally rise to the surface.

stir-fry—To cook small pieces of vegetables, tofu, or other foods in a small amount of vegetable oil over high heat, stirring constantly

Special Ingredients

baking powder—A powder used in baking to lighten dough or batter

bamboo shoots—Tender, fleshy yellow sprouts from bamboo canes. They can be bought canned, whole, or thinly sliced.

basil—A rich, fragrant herb used fresh or dried in cooking

bulgur—Kernels of wheat that have been steamed, dried, and crushed. A similar product called cracked wheat may be used as a substitute.

cardamom—A spice of the ginger family, used whole or ground, that has a rich aroma and gives food a sweet, cool taste

cayenne pepper—Dried red chilies (hot peppers) ground to a fine powder

chickpeas—A type of dried pea with an irregular texture and a nutlike flavor. Chickpeas are also called garbanzo beans.

cinnamon—A spice made from the bark of a tree in the laurel family. It is available ground and in sticks.

coriander—An herb used as flavoring and as a decorative garnish. Dried, powdered coriander is used in curries.

cornstarch—A fine, white starch made from corn, commonly used to thicken sauces and gravies

cumin—The seeds of an herb used whole or ground to give food a pungent, slightly hot flavor

curry powder—A combination of several ground spices, often including cumin and turmeric

feta cheese—A crumbly white cheese made from goat's milk

garlic—A bulbous herb whose distinctive flavor is used in many dishes. Each piece or bulb can be broken up into several small sections called cloves. Before chopping a clove of garlic, remove its papery skin.

garlic powder—Dehydrated garlic in a powder form

ginger root—The knobby, light brown root of a tropical plant, used to flavor food. To use fresh ginger root, slice off the amount called for, peel off the skin with the side of a spoon, and grate the flesh. Freeze the rest of the root for future use. Fresh ginger has a very zippy taste, so use it sparingly. (Do not substitute dried ground ginger in a recipe calling for fresh ginger, as the taste is very different.)

halva—In the Middle East, a sweet candy of crushed nuts or sesame seeds in honey syrup. A dessert called halva is also eaten in India, where it may include butter and grated vegetables.

matzo—Crisp, unleavened bread

mushrooms, dried—Many types of mushrooms are available dried at groceries and specialty markets. Black, oyster, and wood ear mushrooms are a few common varieties. Before dried mushrooms can be used, they must be soaked in warm water for 15 to 20 minutes.

oregano—The dried leaves, whole or ground, of a rich and fragrant herb that is used as a seasoning in cooking

peppercorns—The berries of an East Indian plant. Peppercorns are used both whole and ground to flavor food.

rice noodles—Long, very thin noodles made from rice flour

soy sauce—A dark brown sauce made from soybeans and other ingredients, used extensively in Asian cooking

thyme—A fragrant herb used fresh or dried to season foods

tofu—A processed curd made from soybeans

turmeric—An aromatic East Indian herb

yeast—An ingredient used in cooking to make dough rise and cause liquid to ferment. Yeast is available in either small, white cakes called compressed yeast or in granular form called active dry yeast.

Healthy and Low-Fat Cooking Tips

Many modern cooks are concerned about preparing healthy, low-fat meals. Fortunately, there are simple ways to reduce the fat content of most dishes. Here are a few general tips for adapting the recipes in this book. Throughout the book, you'll also find specific suggestions for individual recipes—and don't worry, they'll still taste delicious!

Many recipes call for butter or oil to sauté vegetables. Using oil instead of butter lowers saturated fat right away, but you can also reduce the amount of oil you use. You can also substitute a low-fat or nonfat cooking spray for oil. Sprinkling a little salt on vegetables brings out their natural juices, so less oil is needed. It's also a good idea to use a small, nonstick frying pan if you decide to use less oil than the recipe calls for.

Another common substitution for butter is margarine. Before making this substitution, consider the recipe. If it is a dessert, it's often best to use butter. Margarine may noticeably change the taste or consistency of the food.

Cheese and other dairy products, such as cream, milk, and sour cream, are common sources of unwanted fat. Many cheeses are available in reduced fat or nonfat varieties, but keep in mind that these varieties often don't melt as well. Another easy way to reduce the amount of fat from cheese is simply to use less of it! To avoid losing flavor, you might try using a stronger-tasting cheese. Another easy way to trim fat from a recipe is to use skim milk in place of cream, whole milk, or 2 percent milk. In recipes that call for sour cream, try substituting low-fat or nonfat sour cream, or plain yogurt.

There are many ways to prepare meals that are good for you and still taste great. As you become a more experienced cook, try experimenting with recipes and substitutions to find the methods that work best for you.

METRIC CONVERSIONS

Cooks in the United States measure both liquid and solid ingredients using standard containers based on the 8-ounce cup and the tablespoon. These measurements are based on volume, while the metric system of measurement is based on both weight (for solids) and volume (for liquids). To convert from U.S. fluid tablespoons, ounces, quarts, and so forth to metric liters is a straightforward conversion, using the chart below. However, since solids have different weights—one cup of rice does not weigh the same as one cup of grated cheese, for example—many cooks who use the metric system have kitchen scales to weigh different ingredients. The chart below will give you a good starting point for basic conversions to the metric system.

MASS (weight)

1 ounce (oz.)	=	28.0 grams (g)
8 ounces	=	227.0 grams
1 pound (lb.) or 16 ounces	=	0.45 kilograms (kg)
2.2 pounds	=	1.0 kilogram

LIQUID VOLUME

1 teaspoon (tsp.)	=	5.0 milliliters (ml)
1 tablespoon (tbsp.)	=	15.0 milliliters
1 fluid ounce (oz.)	=	30.0 milliliters
1 cup (c.)	=	240 milliliters
1 pint (pt.)	=	480 milliliters
1 quart (qt.)	=	0.95 liters (l)
1 gallon (gal.)	=	3.80 liters

LENGTH

¼ inch (in.)	=	0.6 centimeters (cm)
½ inch	=	1.25 centimeters
1 inch	=	2.5 centimeters

TEMPERATURE

212°F	=	100°C (boiling point of water)
225°F	=	110°C
250°F	=	120°C
275°F	=	135°C
300°F	=	150°C
325°F	=	160°C
350°F	=	180°C
375°F	=	190°C
400°F	=	200°C

(To convert temperature in Fahrenheit to Celsius, subtract 32 and multiply by .56)

PAN SIZES

8-inch cake pan	=	20 x 4-centimeter cake pan
9-inch cake pan	=	23 x 3.5-centimeter cake pan
11 x 7-inch baking pan	=	28 x 18-centimeter baking pan
13 x 9-inch baking pan	=	32.5 x 23-centimeter baking pan
9 x 5-inch loaf pan	=	23 x 13-centimeter loaf pan
2-quart casserole	=	2-liter casserole

An International Table

People all over the globe sit down to enjoy tasty, nutritious vegetarian meals every day. Whether kneeling at a traditional, low Japanese dinner table, at an outdoor meal in Africa or India, or sitting at a table adorned with fresh flowers and linen in Poland, families and friends around the world enjoy coming together to share a meal. Using your creativity as a cook and sampling the wide selection of international vegetarian dishes can add new tastes to your table. Whether you choose to mix and match dishes of different origins or to serve an entire meal from the same area of the world, you can also add flair to your table with all sorts of details. If you are serving a Chinese or Vietnamese dish, invite your guests to use chopsticks. If your meal includes African or Indian breads, abandon utensils altogether and use the delicious warm bread to scoop up food. To dress up a French- or Italian-inspired meal, cover your table with a fresh white cloth. But whatever you serve, and however you adorn your table, take time to enjoy preparing and eating your meal.

The groundnuts (peanuts) used to make this African sauce are rich in protein. (Recipe on page 42.) Groundnut sauce can be served with chapatis (recipe on page 28) or over rice (recipe on page 32).

A Vegetarian Menu

Below are suggestions for two international vegetarian meals, along with shopping lists of the items necessary to prepare these meals. Remember that the only rule is to provide both variety and harmony. Choose dishes with textures and flavors that are different but complementary, and you'll have a complete meal that is delicious and satisfying.

LUNCH

Stuffed tomatoes with feta cheese

Bulgur salad

Groundnut sauce over rice

SHOPPING LIST:

Produce

9 medium-sized tomatoes
2 bunches scallions
1 large bunch fresh parsley
1 bunch fresh mint
1 small head lettuce
1 medium onion
1 small eggplant

Dairy/Eggs

3 oz. feta cheese

Canned/Bottled/Boxed

olive oil
vegetable oil
2 c. bulgur
lemon juice
4 oz. smooth unsweetened
    peanut butter

Miscellaneous

bread crumbs
white rice
salt
pepper

DINNER

Creamy pumpkin soup

Brown fava beans

Rice

Grilled veggies on skewers with Turkish marinade

Mango with cinnamon

SHOPPING LIST:

Produce

1 large and 1 small onion
fresh parsley
1 bulb garlic
2 lemons
2 tomatoes
1–2 lbs. (total) of various
    fresh veggies for grilling
    (zucchini, new potatoes,
    red onions, cherry
    tomatoes, etc.)
2–3 mangoes (or a 1-lb. can
    of mangoes)

Dairy/Eggs

1 stick butter or margarine
16 oz. half-and-half or whole
    milk
4 oz. sour cream
2 eggs
4 oz. plain yogurt

Canned/Bottled/Boxed

16 oz. canned pumpkin
20 oz. canned vegetable
    broth
18 oz. canned fava beans
olive oil
lemon juice

Miscellaneous

white rice
cinnamon
curry powder
thyme
shredded coconut
salt
pepper
wooden skewers

Breads and Staples

What diners think of as breads and staples varies tremendously from country to country. Plump, crusty loaves of bread are familiar sights on tables in North America and Europe. Most Indian breads, on the other hand, have no leavening agent like yeast, so they do not rise when they are cooked. Chapati, the most popular kind of Indian bread, is a flat, pancake-shaped bread that looks something like a Mexican tortilla. Like tortillas, chapati are cooked on a very hot, ungreased griddle. Chapati are also eaten in the African countries of Kenya, Tanzania, and Uganda, but there they are usually fried in oil. Rice is the primary staple in most Asian countries, and many families eat steaming hot rice with every meal, while wheat breads are less common. Rice is also a common dish in South America, the Caribbean, and Africa.

Both chapatis (bottom, recipe on page 28) and rye bread (top, recipe on page 30) are sure to make any meal complete.

Unleavened Whole Wheat Bread / *Chapatis* (India)

Served warm and fresh, chapatis complement a spicy curry and a cool yogurt dip. They are also delicious with rice and bean dishes.

2½ c. whole wheat flour

2 tbsp. butter or margarine

1 tsp. salt

1 c. lukewarm water

1. Put 2 c. flour into a large mixing bowl.

2. Cut butter into small pieces. Make a hollow in the center of the flour and add butter. Rub butter into flour with your fingertips until mixture looks like large bread crumbs.

3. Mix salt into water. Add enough water, a little at a time, to flour mixture to make a firm (but not stiff) dough.

4. Knead dough in bowl for about 5 or 10 minutes. Cover bowl with a damp cloth and let stand at room temperature for at least 1 hour.

5. Divide dough into pieces about the size of walnuts. Roll each piece into a smooth ball with your hands.

6. Sprinkle remaining ½ c. flour onto a flat surface. With a rolling pin, roll out each ball until it resembles a thin pancake, about ⅛-inch thick.

7. Heat an ungreased heavy skillet or griddle over medium-high heat. When the skillet is hot, place one chapati in the center. When small brown spots appear on the bottom, and the edges begin to curl up (in about 1 minute), turn the chapati over with a spatula. Cook chapati for about 2 minutes, or until small brown spots appear on bottom.*

8. Continue cooking chapatis, one at a time. Wrap the cooked ones in a towel to keep them warm.

9. Brush cooked chapatis with butter and serve warm.

Preparation time: 1 hour 35 minutes
Cooking time: 30 minutes
Makes 12 to 15 chapatis

---

* To make a deep-fried Indian bread called puri, heat 1 tbsp. of oil in the skillet over medium-high heat for 1 minute. Place a dough circle in the oil. Using a spatula, carefully splash hot oil from the pan onto the puri while frying. This technique will cook the top side and puff up the dough. (It may be necessary to add a little oil to the pan for each new puri.) Fry for about 2 minutes, or until golden brown on both sides. Remove from skillet, drain on paper towels, and serve immediately.

Rye Bread/Rzhanoi Khleb (Russia)

This hearty dark bread is delicious with hot soups and stews. It also makes good sandwich bread.

2 packages active dry yeast
   (4½ tsp.)

1 c. warm water (105 to 115°F)

⅓ c. dark corn syrup

4½ to 5½ c. dark rye flour

2 tsp. salt

1. In a large bowl, dissolve yeast in 1 c. warm water. Stir in corn syrup and set aside for 5 minutes until yeast mixture foams. If, after 5 minutes, yeast mixture has not started to foam, discard the mixture and try again.

2. Add 2½ c. flour to the yeast mixture, a little at a time, and beat with a spoon until smooth. Stir in salt.

3. Set bowl in a warm place, cover with a cloth towel (not terry cloth), and let rise for 30 minutes.

4. When dough is risen, add 2 to 3 more cups flour, a half cup at a time, stirring after each addition. When dough becomes difficult to stir, turn out onto a floured surface and knead in flour with your hands until dough is stiff but still slightly sticky. Form dough into a ball.

5. Wash and dry bowl. Place dough in bowl, cover with a cloth towel, and set in a warm place. Let rise again for 2½ to 3 hours, or until dough almost doubles.

6. Turn dough out onto floured surface and, with floured hands, form into a loaf. Place loaf in a well-greased 9- by 5-inch loaf pan, cover tightly with plastic wrap, and return to warm place to rise for 1 hour.

7. Preheat oven to 350°F.

8. Bake loaf for 30 to 35 minutes. (Bread will not brown much.)

Preparation time: 45 minutes
Rising time: 4 to 4½ hours
Baking time: 30 to 35 minutes
Makes 1 loaf

*The secret to making good rye bread is not to add too much flour and to be patient enough to let the bread rise fully.

Rice

Rice is the staple food in much of Asia, but cooks in different countries may prefer different types of rice and use slightly different cooking techniques. For example, this is a recipe for Japanese short-grain rice (gohan). However, long-grain rice is more popular for most dishes in China, Vietnamese diners prefer extra-long grain, and Thai cooks almost always choose jasmine rice.

2 c. short-grain white rice, uncooked

2½ c. cold water

1. Wash rice in a pan with cold water and drain in a sieve. Repeat until water runs clear.

2. In a covered heavy pot or saucepan, bring rice and 2½ c. water quickly to a boil. Lower heat and simmer until all water is absorbed (about 30 minutes).

3. Turn off heat and let rice steam for another 10 minutes.

Preparation time: 10 minutes
Cooking time: 40 minutes
Serves 6 to 8

*In China, congee, or jook, is a rice porridge that is commonly eaten for breakfast. Basic congee is very simple to make. In a deep saucepan, combine 1 c. short-grain rice and 8 c. cold water. Bring to a boil, cover, and reduce heat. Simmer for about 1½ hours, stirring every now and then to keep rice from sticking to the bottom of the pan. Just about anything can be added to congee, from veggies to dried fruit and nuts. To quickly spice up this basic recipe, try topping it with chopped scallions and fresh, thinly sliced ginger.

Main Dishes

Eliminating a central, meat-based dish from the menu allows the vegetarian cook to create a varied, versatile meal out of a combination of many different dishes, some of which would be considered side dishes on a nonvegetarian menu. Some of the recipes in this section are not meant to be entrées on their own. For example, Lebanese *tabbouleh* might not always be enough for a main course. However, when served together with another dish or two, it can form part of a delicious lunch or a light summer dinner. An Italian pizza fresh from the oven, on the other hand, is a meal in itself. Or try serving a hot creamy soup with bread, cheese, and a basic green salad, for a quick and easy meal that is also complete and satisfying. Use your imagination! The possibilities of a vegetarian menu are almost endless.

Pizza, an Italian favorite, can be adapted to your personal tastes. (Recipe on page 48.)

Stuffed Tomatoes with Feta Cheese/
Domates me Feta (Greece)

Fine, fresh vegetables are found throughout Greece. For this recipe, it is important to use the reddest, ripest tomatoes available.

4 medium-sized ripe tomatoes*

2 tbsp. finely chopped scallions

2 tbsp. finely chopped fresh parsley

½ c. (about 3 oz.) finely crumbled
    feta cheese

¼ c. bread crumbs

3 tbsp. olive oil

1. Carefully cut tops off tomatoes. Using a spoon, carefully scoop out pulp and seeds. Save pulp and discard seeds.

2. Coarsely chop the tomato pulp.

3. Preheat oven to 350°F.

4. In a small bowl, combine tomato pulp with scallions, parsley, feta cheese, bread crumbs, and olive oil.

5. Spoon mixture into the hollowed-out tomatoes. Place tomatoes right side up in an 8- by 8-inch baking pan and bake 15 minutes.

6. Serve stuffed tomatoes steaming hot.

*If your tomatoes aren't quite ripe (pinkish-orange instead of bright red), place them in a brown paper bag and keep in a cupboard or other dark place for a day or two to ripen.

Preparation time: 35 minutes
Cooking time: 15 minutes
Serves 4

Fresh tomatoes and feta cheese conjure up a delicious taste of summertime in Greece.

Bulgur Salad / *Tabbouleh* (*Lebanon*)

2 c. bulgur

1 bunch green onions, chopped (about ½ c.)

1 c. coarsely chopped fresh parsley

½ c. coarsely chopped fresh mint leaves

¾ c. olive oil

½ c. lemon juice

salt and pepper to taste

3 tomatoes, peeled*, seeded**, and chopped

1. Place bulgur in a small bowl and add enough warm water to cover the bulgur by about ¼ inch. Set aside to soak for 15 minutes.

2. Drain bulgur in a sieve or fine strainer. Use your hands to squeeze out any extra water.

3. Place bulgur in a large mixing bowl and add onions. Stir well. Add parsley and mint and toss gently.

4. In a small bowl, combine olive oil, lemon juice, salt, and pepper. Pour dressing over salad and gently stir in the tomatoes.

Preparation time: 35 minutes
Serves 4 to 6

*To peel a tomato, place it in a small saucepan of boiling water for about 1 minute. Remove with a slotted spoon and cool until the tomato is warm but no longer hot. Use a small paring knife to peel off the skin. It will come off easily.

** To seed a tomato, cut the peeled tomato in half and use a paring knife to cut out the seeds.

Creamy Pumpkin Soup (Australia)

Nearly every Australian family has its own version of this delicious golden soup. They usually make it with hard-shelled winter squash, which they call pumpkin.

¼ c. butter or margarine*

1 large onion, peeled and chopped

½ tsp. curry powder

1 16-oz. can pumpkin (2 c.)

¼ tsp. salt

2 c. half-and-half*

2½ c. vegetable broth

⅓ c. sour cream*

⅛ tsp. cinnamon

2 tsp. minced parsley

1. Melt butter in a medium-sized saucepan. Add chopped onion and, stirring frequently, cook until soft but not brown. Add curry powder and cook 1 to 2 minutes longer.

2. Place curried onion in a food processor or blender. Add pumpkin and salt and process until smooth. Add half-and-half and process again until smooth.

3. Pour pumpkin mixture back into saucepan and stir in vegetable broth. Heat soup slowly over low heat, stirring occasionally. Meanwhile, stir cinnamon and minced parsley into the sour cream.

4. Serve soup steaming hot with a dollop of seasoned sour cream in each bowl.

Preparation and cooking time: 30 to 40 minutes
Serves 6

*For a lighter soup, use half the amount of butter, evaporated skim milk instead of half-and-half, and low-fat or non-fat sour cream instead of regular.

Potato-and-Leek Soup/
Potage Parmentier (France)

This creamy soup, along with French bread, makes a delicious and filling meal. Leftover soup keeps well in the refrigerator and can be reheated the next day. (Make sure that you don't boil the soup because boiling will make the dairy curdle, or form lumps.) This soup can also be eaten cold. The French call the cold version vichyssoise.

3 medium-sized potatoes, peeled and sliced ⅛-inch thick

3 medium-sized leeks, washed thoroughly and sliced ⅛-inch thick (do not use the tough, dark green part), or 3 medium-sized yellow onions, thinly sliced

3 10¾-oz. cans vegetable broth

1 vegetable-broth can of cold water

½ c. whipping cream (add up to an extra ½ c. milk if you like your soup thin)*

2 tbsp. butter or margarine*

2 tsp. salt

¼ tsp. pepper

chopped chives to garnish

1. Combine potatoes, leeks or onions, vegetable broth, and water in a large heavy pot or saucepan.

2. Cover and bring to a boil over medium-high heat. Reduce heat and simmer 35 to 45 minutes, or until vegetables are tender.

3. Without draining off broth, mash vegetables in the pan with a vegetable (potato) masher until they are fairly smooth. (If they do not mash easily, soup has not cooked long enough. Let it simmer 10 to 15 minutes longer.)

4. Add cream, butter, salt, and pepper. Heat soup just to the boiling point. (Do not boil.)

5. Serve in bowls and sprinkle each serving with chives.

Preparation time: 10 to 15 minutes
Cooking time: 1 to 1¼ hours
Serves 4 to 5

*To lower the fat content of this soup, substitute evaporated skim milk for the whipping cream and eliminate the butter.

Groundnut Sauce (East and West Africa)

2 tbsp. vegetable oil

1 medium onion, peeled and chopped

2 medium tomatoes, cut into bite-sized pieces

1 small eggplant, with or without peel, cut into bite-sized pieces

½ c. smooth unsweetened peanut butter (available in the health food section of many supermarkets)

¼ c. water

1. In a large frying pan, heat oil over medium heat for 1 minute. Add onions and sauté until transparent. Add tomatoes and cook for 5 minutes. Add eggplant and cook for 5 minutes more.

2. In a small bowl, combine peanut butter and ¼ c. water and stir to make a paste. Add to tomato mixture and stir well.

3. Reduce heat to medium-low and simmer, uncovered, for 10 minutes, or until eggplant is tender.

Preparation time: 30 minutes
Serves 4 to 6

Yogurt and Bananas/Kela ka Raita (India)

1½ c. (12 oz.) plain yogurt

2 large bananas, peeled and sliced

¼ c. flaked coconut

1 green chili, finely chopped

1 tsp. lemon juice

¼ tsp. ground coriander

¼ tsp. cinnamon

¼ tsp. salt

1 tsp. fresh coriander leaves

1. In a medium mixing bowl, beat yogurt until smooth. Stir in bananas, coconut, chili, lemon juice, coriander, cinnamon, and salt. Cover bowl and chill at least 1 hour.

2. Just before serving, sprinkle chopped coriander leaves over raita.

Preparation time: 15 minutes
(plus 1 hour to chill)
Serves 4

Spanish Omelette/ *Tortilla Española (Spain)*

A tortilla, or omelette, appears almost daily in a Spanish home. It can be eaten as a main dish at a light supper or as a side dish at the big midday meal, and slices of it can be served as tapas (appetizers). Good hot or cold, the tortilla is usually served hot and the leftovers are refrigerated for a snack.

¼ c. olive oil*

I large onion, minced

I large potato, minced

¼ tsp. salt

5 large eggs, beaten

I tbsp. olive oil

1. Heat olive oil in a frying pan over moderate heat. Add onion and potato and sprinkle with salt. Cook until soft, but not brown, stirring occasionally.

2. Add about ⅓ of the beaten egg. Using a spatula, lift up omelette at the edges and center to allow egg to run under potato and onion. Repeat this procedure until all the egg has been added.

3. When egg is firm but still slightly moist (not runny) and golden on the bottom, run the spatula under omelette to loosen it from the pan. Then place a plate over the top and flip omelette onto the plate. (You may want to have someone help you with this.)

4. Add another tbsp. olive oil to the pan and slide omelette back in, brown side up. Continue cooking omelette over moderate heat until golden on the other side.

*The nutlike flavor of the Spanish omelette comes from slowly cooking the potato and onion in olive oil. This unique taste is lost if any other kind of oil is used.

Preparation time: 10 to 15 minutes
Cooking time: 15 to 25 minutes
Serves 2 to 4

Grilled Veggies on Skewers

Creative cooks around the world have been grilling different types of food on skewers for generations. Japanese kushiyaki, Greek souvlaki, and Turkish shish kebab are all variations on this same tasty theme. The recipe below gives suggestions for a variety of ingredients, along with several different marinades to evoke the flavor of different international cuisines. Feel free to be creative and try your own combinations of ingredients and seasoning!

8 wooden skewers that have been soaked in water for at least 30 minutes

1–2 lbs. of any combination of the following ingredients, cut into bite-sized pieces if necessary:

cauliflower florets

cherry tomatoes

eggplant

firm tofu

green, red, or yellow bell peppers

mushrooms

new potatoes

red onion

yellow squash

zucchini

Japanese Marinade:

¼ c. soy sauce

2 tbsp. sugar

1 tbsp. fresh ginger root, grated

Greek Marinade:

½ c. olive oil

6 tbsp. fresh lemon juice

2 cloves garlic, crushed

1 tbsp. fresh oregano, chopped

salt and pepper to taste

Turkish Marinade:

1 c. olive oil

¼ c. plain yogurt

1 small onion, finely chopped

1 tbsp. lemon juice

1 tbsp. thyme

salt and pepper to taste

1. Prepare your choice of marinade by combining all ingredients and mixing well to blend.

2. Thread desired grilling ingredients onto skewers. Place skewers in a long shallow dish.

3. Pour marinade over skewered veggies, cover, and marinate for 1 to 2 hours at room temperature.

4. Have an experienced cook start a charcoal or gas grill, or preheat the oven to "broil."

5. Remove skewers from marinade and let excess liquid drip off. Grill or broil skewers for 6–12 minutes, turning every few minutes, until lightly charred and cooked through. Watch carefully, as different ingredients may take different amounts of time to cook.

6. Remove skewers to a serving platter and pour any extra marinade over skewers. Serve hot, with rice if desired.

Preparation time: 30 minutes
Marination time: 1 hour
Cooking time: 6 to 12 minutes
Serves 4

Pizza (Italy)

Pizza is an old favorite that has dozens of vegetarian possibilities. One of the most popular pizzas in Italy is Pizza Margherita, topped with the colors of the Italian flag: fresh red tomatoes, green basil leaves, and creamy white mozzarella.

Pizza ingredients:

1 envelope active dry yeast

1 c. warm water

½ tsp. salt

2 tbsp. olive oil

2½ c. all-purpose flour

pizza sauce (recipe follows)

8 oz. mozzarella cheese, grated

desired pizza toppings, cut into bite-sized pieces (suggestions follow)

1. Dissolve yeast in 1 c. warm water. Stir in salt and oil. Gradually stir in flour. Beat vigorously 20 strokes. Let dough rest about 5 minutes.

2. Put dough in a warm place, cover with a damp towel, and let rise until double in size (about 45 minutes).

3. Punch dough down with your fist to let out the air. Divide dough in half.

4. Lightly grease 2 baking sheets or 2 10-inch pizza pans. With floured fingers, pat each half of the dough into a 10-inch circle. Build up edges of pizzas with your fingers to keep sauce from running off.

5. Spread pizza sauce over dough. Sprinkle with grated cheese and your favorite toppings.

6. Bake at 425°F for 20 to 25 minutes. Let pizzas stand at least 5 minutes before cutting.

Preparation time: 15 minutes
Rising time: 30 to 45 minutes
Baking time: 20 to 25 minutes
Serves 4 to 6

No-cook pizza sauce:

1 6-oz. can tomato paste

1 16-oz. can chopped tomatoes

2 cloves garlic, minced

1 tsp. oregano

1 tsp. basil

1 tsp. olive oil

¼ c. minced onion

1 green pepper, cleaned out and
minced (optional)

1. In a large bowl, mix all ingredients together with a fork.

2. Spoon sauce onto unbaked pizza crust. Add topping and bake as directed in step 6 on page 48.

Preparation time: 15 minutes
Enough for 2 pizzas

Pizza toppings:

artichoke hearts	mushrooms
basil, oregano, or other herbs	onions
broccoli	pineapple
cheddar, feta, or other cheeses	potatoes
fresh or sun-dried tomatoes	roasted garlic
green or black olives	spinach
green or sweet red peppers	zucchini

Sweet Potatoes with Peanuts/
Khoai lang nau (Vietnam)

2 c. water

½ c. sugar

2 medium sweet potatoes, peeled
and cut into chunks

½ tsp. salt

¼ tsp. pepper

¼ c. chopped roasted peanuts

1. In a large saucepan, bring water and sugar to a boil over high heat.

2. Add sweet potatoes and cover. Turn heat to low and simmer for 10 minutes, or until tender.

3. In a colander, drain sweet potatoes and place in a serving bowl. Add salt and pepper and stir. Sprinkle with peanuts and serve hot.

Preparation time: 5 to 10 minutes
Cooking time: 20 to 25 minutes
Serves 4

Steamed Tofu/Dau hui hap (Vietnam)

1 1-lb. package firm-style tofu,
cut into chunks

2 tbsp. soy sauce

½ c. chopped scallions

¼ tsp. salt

¼ tsp. pepper

¼ tsp. red pepper flakes

1. Place all ingredients in a heat-resistant bowl and mix well.

2. Place ½ c. water in steamer and bring to a boil. Place bowl with tofu into steamer. Cover and steam over medium heat for 25 minutes. Serve hot, with rice or plain.

Preparation time: 10 to 15 minutes
Cooking time: 35 to 40 minutes
Serves 4

Sweet potatoes with peanuts (top) and steamed tofu (bottom) are classic vegetarian dishes in Vietnam.

Curried Chickpeas/*Channa Dal (India)*

Dal is the Hindi word for pulses, those versatile beans, lentils, and peas that are such an important part of the Indian diet. Most Indians have some kind of dal at almost every meal.

1½ c. (12 oz.) chickpeas, washed and drained

5 c. water

1 tsp. ground turmeric

½ tsp. ground cumin

1 tsp. ground coriander

½ tsp. cayenne pepper (optional)

3 tbsp. butter or margarine

1 tsp. cumin seed

1 medium onion, chopped

1 clove garlic, chopped

1 tbsp. grated fresh ginger

2 tbsp. chopped fresh coriander leaves

1. Put chickpeas in a bowl. Add enough cold water to cover and soak overnight.

2. To cook, drain chickpeas. Place chickpeas, water, turmeric, cumin, coriander, and cayenne in a heavy saucepan and bring to a boil over medium-high heat. Reduce heat to low, cover pan, and simmer for about 1 hour.

3. In a large saucepan, melt butter over medium heat. Add cumin seed and cook for 1 minute. Add the onion, garlic, and ginger and cook for about 5 minutes, stirring frequently, or until onion turns golden brown.

4. Add chickpeas and cooking liquid to onion mixture. Turn heat to high and bring to a boil, stirring constantly. Cover pan, reduce heat to low, and simmer 30 minutes, or until chickpeas are tender but not mushy. Mix well.

5. Place chickpeas in a serving dish and sprinkle with coriander leaves.

*Eaten with a starchy food like bread or rice and a milk product such as yogurt, dal forms the basis of a well-balanced diet.

Preparation time: 15 minutes (plus overnight soaking)
Cooking time: 1½ hours
Serves 6 to 8

Brown Fava Beans/Ful Medames (Egypt)

Often called the national dish of Egypt, ful medames is a versatile dish that can be prepared very simply and then seasoned to each individual diner's taste.

2 eggs

1 18-oz. can brown fava beans, drained*

3 cloves fresh garlic, crushed

¼ c. fresh parsley, chopped

2 lemons, cut into wedges

2 tomatoes, chopped

olive oil

salt and pepper

1. Place eggs in a medium saucepan and cover with cold water. Place over medium heat until boiling, reduce heat, and simmer for 15 minutes. Drain water from saucepan and run cold water over eggs until they are cool.

2. Peel cooked eggs, cut into halves, and set aside.

3. Place beans in a large saucepan and heat over medium heat until heated through and steaming slightly, about 6 to 8 minutes.

4. Serve beans in individual bowls. Place eggs, garlic, parsley, lemons, tomatoes, olive oil, and salt and pepper on table and allow diners to garnish and season as they like.

*If you have the time, buy 1 lb. dried beans and soak them overnight. Then, in place of step 3, simmer for 1 to 2 hours (until tender) in plenty of water with a handful of red lentils and a pinch of salt.

Preparation and cooking time: 40 to 45 minutes
Serves 4

Ful medames can be served hot or cold and makes a great choice for any meal of the day. In Cairo, Egypt, street vendors sell this favorite to hungry passersby.

Desserts

Some diners may think that eating according to a vegetarian diet means giving up great-tasting foods. Just a nibble of the delicious desserts in this section is enough to correct that idea. Most sweet dishes are perfectly adapted to a vegetarian menu, and although they might not be served on a daily basis, they make a wonderful addition to a healthy meal.

In many cultures, especially in warm and tropical climates, a typical dessert consists of little more than fresh fruit. Eaten alone or as part of a more elaborate dish, fruit is a great way to add important vitamins and nutrients to the day's menu.

Other popular desserts around the world are cookies, biscuits, and sweet breads. These treats are often enjoyed with a hot beverage such as coffee, tea, or hot chocolate. For holidays and special occasions, richer, fancier desserts provide a festive finale to any meal.

Nothing tops off a delicious dinner like delicate French crepes with fresh strawberries and powdered sugar. (Recipe on page 62.)

Mango with Cinnamon/Mango Canela (Mexico)

Topped with coconut and cinnamon, mango canela is a flavorful and refreshing treat.

2 to 3 fresh mangoes, or a 1-lb. can of mangoes

¼ c. shredded coconut

1 tsp. cinnamon

1. If using fresh mangoes, allow ½ mango per person. To cut up a fresh mango, place the fruit on a cutting board. Slice down on each side of the mango, close to the large, flat seed in the center. You will have two rounded sections of fruit and one flat section with the seed. Place a round section on the cutting board, cut side up. Slicing down to the skin but not through it, make cuts across the section about every half inch. Turn fruit 90 degrees and make another set of cuts. Hold the mango section in both hands. Push on the skin with your fingers and turn the section inside out. The flesh will separate on the cuts you made, and you'll be able to pick or slice mango cubes off the skin. Repeat with other side. Next, peel the middle section. Carefully slice the flesh from the seed.

2. Refrigerate mangoes overnight to chill thoroughly.

3. To serve, place mango in a dessert dish or fruit cup. Top with coconut and sprinkle lightly with cinnamon.

Preparation time: 15 minutes (plus overnight refrigeration)
Serves 4 to 6

58

Butter Cookies/*Kourabiéthes* (Greece)

Butter cookies are a favorite dessert year-round in Greece.

2½ c. all-purpose flour

I tsp. baking powder

¼ tsp. salt

I c. (2 sticks) butter, softened

½ c. sugar

I egg

½ tsp. vanilla extract

¼ tsp. almond extract

powdered sugar for sprinkling

1. Preheat oven to 350°F.

2. In a small bowl, combine flour, baking powder, and salt.

3. In a large bowl, beat together butter, sugar, and egg until light and fluffy. Add vanilla and almond extracts and mix well. Add flour mixture to butter mixture and mix until well blended.*

4. With your hands, form dough into balls, crescents, or S-shapes, using about ½ tbsp. at a time.

5. Place cookies 2 inches apart on an ungreased cookie sheet. Put on middle oven rack and bake 15 minutes, or until barely brown around the edges.

6. Remove cookies from sheet with a spatula and cool on a wire rack for 5 minutes.

7. Use a flour sifter to sift powdered sugar over cookies.

*For a tasty variation, add ½ c. of chopped blanched almonds to the soft dough.

Preparation time: 35 minutes
Cooking and cooling time: 20 minutes
Makes about 3 dozen cookies

Serve these bite-sized delights with coffee or hot chocolate for a sweet treat.

Crepes with Strawberries/
Crêpes aux Fraises (France)

Crepes are an old standby in France. Not just for dessert, crepes can also be made with unsweetened batter and wrapped around ingredients such as veggies and cheese to provide a filling main dish.

Crepe batter:

2 eggs

½ c. all-purpose flour

1 tbsp. sugar

½ c. milk

⅛ c. water

½ tbsp. melted butter

Filling:

3 c. fresh, sliced strawberries*

⅓ c. granulated sugar

8 oz. (1 c.) cottage cheese

8 oz. (1 c.) sour cream

½ c. powdered sugar

1. Beat eggs in a bowl. Add a little bit of the flour and sugar. Use an electric mixer or whisk to combine. Then add a little bit of the milk and water. Mix. Repeat until all of the flour, sugar, milk, and water have been added. Then beat with a whisk or electric mixer until smooth.

2. Beat in melted butter.

3. Chill batter at least 1 hour. In the meantime, combine strawberries and granulated sugar. Set aside.

4. Beat cottage cheese in a blender or with an electric mixer until smooth. Add sour cream and powdered sugar and stir well.

5. When batter is chilled, heat a crepe pan on medium-high heat. Pour batter into the pan as you would to make a pancake. Swirl batter to coat the entire bottom of the pan and cook for about 2 minutes, or until the bottom of the crepe is firm.

6. Use a fork to gently lift crepe from pan. Quickly flip the crepe over and cook for 1 minute, or until crepe just starts to brown. Remove to a plate and repeat with remaining batter.

7. Use about ⅔ of fruit and creamy mixture to fill crepes. Fold crepes over. Top with remaining fruit and creamy mixture, or top with fruit and powdered sugar.

Preparation time: 45 minutes
(plus 1 hour to chill batter)
Cooking time: 10 to 15 minutes
Makes 10 to 12 crepes

*These crepes can easily be filled with other kinds of fresh fruit. Try using 3 c. of blueberries or sliced peaches instead of strawberries.

Holiday and Festival Food

Whatever the country and whatever the celebration, special occasions call for special foods. Many holiday recipes require more time and more ingredients than everyday foods, but cooks around the world think it's worth the extra effort to make these dishes just right. In Japan, for example, where food preparation is considered an art every day of the year, holiday foods are even more carefully arranged and presented. Polish cooks spend most of Easter weekend getting ready for the Easter Sunday feast. In Vietnam, the traditional New Year's cake takes many hours to prepare. African Muslim cooks are busy at Eid al-Fitr making enough special dishes to be enjoyed throughout the three-day celebration.

The recipes in this section offer a sampling of vegetarian dishes served on special occasions in different countries. Try these—and discover others—to get an international taste of the holidays.

The Passover matzo layer cake is the perfect end to a meatless meal—or a festive treat on its own. (Recipe on page 67.)

New Year's Noodles (China)

Long noodles, a favorite dish at New Year's, are also served at birthdays to ensure long life. In China, New Year's is something like a nationwide birthday party. During this festival, all Chinese people add a year to their age, no matter when they were born.

8 oz. dried rice noodles

12 dried Chinese or oyster
    mushrooms

1 c. vegetable broth

1 tbsp. soy sauce

1 tbsp. cornstarch

1 tsp. sugar

1 tbsp. peanut oil

1 tbsp. minced garlic

2 tsp. minced fresh ginger

1½ c. chopped Chinese cabbage

1½ c. bean sprouts

1 c. sliced bamboo shoots

1 tsp. sesame oil (optional)

1 to 2 scallions, chopped,
    for garnish

1. Prepare noodles according to package directions and set aside.

2. Soak mushrooms in warm water for 20 minutes. Squeeze dry, trim off stems, and cut into bite-sized pieces.

3. While mushrooms are soaking, make sauce by mixing the vegetable broth, soy sauce, cornstarch, and sugar in a small bowl. Set aside.

4. In a skillet or wok, heat peanut oil. Add garlic and ginger and stir-fry until garlic barely begins to brown.

5. Add mushrooms, cabbage, bean sprouts, and bamboo shoots. Stir-fry until tender (about 3 to 4 minutes).

6. Add sauce and noodles to pan. Lower heat, and simmer uncovered for 3 to 5 minutes.

7. Sprinkle with sesame oil, if desired, and toss well.

8. Remove from heat, garnish with scallions, and serve.

Preparation time: 25 minutes
Cooking time: 15 minutes
Serves 4

Passover Matzo Layer Cake/Ugat Matzot (Israel)

For an extra, festive touch, scatter colored candy sprinkles over this cake as a decoration.

6 tbsp. sugar

4 squares unsweetened chocolate

1 c. water

1 stick (¼ lb.) butter or margarine, cut into pieces

6 oz. halva, cut into small pieces*

2 tbsp. cornstarch

6 large matzos

1. In a medium saucepan, combine sugar, chocolate, and water. Cook over medium-high heat, stirring constantly, until chocolate is completely melted and mixture begins to bubble.

2. Add butter and halva. Continue stirring until mixture just begins to boil, then remove pan from heat.

3. In a small bowl, mix cornstarch with 2 tbsp. water and stir into chocolate mixture. Cook over medium heat, stirring until mixture thickens. Remove pan from heat.

4. Put 1 large matzo on a platter large enough to let it lie flat. Spread an even layer of chocolate over matzo. Place another matzo on top. Cover with chocolate. Repeat with remaining matzos, finishing with a layer of chocolate.

5. Refrigerate cake overnight. To serve, cut cake with a sharp knife into 1- by 2-inch rectangles.

*The best halva is made from almonds, but you can also buy sesame and peanut halva. Halva can be purchased at any Greek, Middle Eastern, or Jewish market.

Preparation time: 20 minutes
Refrigeration time: overnight
Serves 10

Bruschetta (Italy)

3 ripe red tomatoes, diced

2 cloves garlic, finely chopped

⅓ c. chopped fresh basil

⅓ c. chopped fresh parsley

½ tsp. each salt and pepper

⅓ c. olive oil

8 ½-inch-thick slices of crusty Italian or French bread

1. Preheat oven to 400°F.

2. Combine all ingredients except bread and set aside.

3. Place bread slices on a cookie sheet and toast in the oven for 5 minutes. Flip slices and toast for 5 more minutes, or until golden brown. Remove and place on a serving plate.

4. Spoon tomato mixture over toasted bread and serve immediately.

Preparation and cooking time: 30 minutes
Serves 4

Christmas Eve Borscht/Wigilijny Barszcz (Poland)

12 medium beets, washed and peeled

1 medium onion, thickly sliced

4 c. water

juice of 1 lemon (about 2 tbsp.)

1 tbsp. sugar

¼ tsp. each salt and pepper

2 c. vegetable stock

1. In a large pot, combine beets, onion, and water. Simmer until beets are tender, about 40 minutes. Add lemon juice, sugar, salt, and pepper. Remove from heat, cover, and refrigerate overnight.

2. Using a slotted spoon, remove and discard beets and onions. Add vegetable stock, and salt and pepper to taste. Heat through and serve hot. Garnish with sour cream and dill.

Preparation time: 20 minutes (plus overnight to chill)
Cooking time: 1 hour
Serves 4 to 6

Index

Photo Acknowledgments

The photographs in this book are reproduced courtesy of: © Wolfgang Kaehler, p. 2–3; © Walter, Louiseann Pietrowicz/September 8th Stock, pp. 4 (both), 5 (left), 6, 14, 26, 33, 34, 37, 51, 55, 56, 60, 69; © AFP/CORBIS, p. 10; © Marc Garanger/ CORBIS, p. 13; © Robert L. and Diane Wolfe, pp. 5 (right), 22, 40, 43, 44, 52, 59, 64.

Cover photos: © Wolfgang Kaehler, front (top); © Walter, Louiseann Pietrowicz/September 8th Stock, front (bottom), spine, back.

The illustrations on pages 7, 15, 23, 27, 29, 31, 32, 35, 36, 38, 39, 45, 52, 54, 57, 61, 63, 65, 67 are by Tim Seeley.